Tack Explained

Horseman's Handbooks

A Horseman's Handbook

Carol Green
Tack Explained

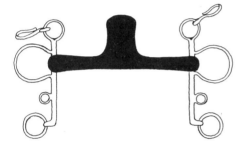

Ward Lock Limited·London

Acknowledgments

We are particularly indebted to master saddler, Walter Kenward, for his expert knowledge and help in checking the manuscript; to Marie Stokes F.B.H.S. for her assistance and technical advice; to Candida Geddes for the benefit of her help in the preparation of this book; to Alison Sherred for her expert knowledge of tack in the United States; to Julia Stiles for additional line drawings; and to Peter Landon, whose colour and black-and-white photographs have so enriched this publication.

© Carol Green 1977

First published in Great Britain in 1977
by Ward Lock Limited, 82 Gower Street,
London WC1E 6EQ, an Egmont Company.

Reprinted 1979, 1982, 1985

Layout by Heather Sherratt
House Editor Eleanor-Mary Cadell
Cover photographs: Peter Loughran

Text filmset in Times New Roman
by Computacomp (UK) Ltd, Fort William, Scotland
Printed and bound in Great Britain by
Hollen Street Press Ltd, Slough

British Library Cataloguing in Publication Data
Green, Carol
  Tack explained.
  1. Harness 2. Saddlery
  I. Title
  636.1'08'37   SF309.9

  ISBN 0-7063-6409-0

Contents

Xenophon, a great horseman of ancient Greece and writer on the art of horsemanship, rode with a curb bit and bridle, but without stirrups.

1 A little history

The bridle first came into being as a result of man's desire to control the horse: he discovered that if he had control of the horse's head he could control the horse. This was first done by tying a piece of rope around the horse's jaws, but as early as the seventh century BC the bridle as we know it today was beginning to take shape: the Assyrians made bridles with metal bits, using a noseband, cheekpiece and throatlatch very similar to modern designs.

The horse used for riding in the Middle Ages was a much heavier animal than the type of horse used today. Bridles, bits and saddles were also more clumsy, and heavier in design. As early as the fourth century BC we have reference made by Xenophon to the first curb and snaffle bit used together – the forerunner of today's double bridle. It is interesting to compare modern saddlery with the original bits, bridles and saddles, and to discover that although today they are generally lighter and smaller, the actual designs have not changed a great deal.

I wonder if you have ever considered how the form of the saddle that you ride in today came about. Horses have been used for riding since before the birth of Christ, and from earliest times man has tried putting something on the horse's back to make his ride more comfortable. The first saddle was simply a cloth placed on the horse's back; then it was padded and quilted, rather like the numnah used today, and in order to prevent the pad from slipping, a strap round the horse's belly was added. As man became more proficient at riding and began to feel at ease on the horse, he started to work up and down hill, moving at faster paces. It became necessary to fit a strap round the horse's chest, and another from the back of the pad to the horse's tail – the first breastplate and crupper. In order to stop him from slipping when riding at faster paces, man put extra padding at the back and front of the pad, forming the first pommel and cantle.

The next invention was the stirrup iron. It was of course very different from present-day designs, but followed the same principles. Riding on long journeys, men felt the need to rest their feet in something, so made loops for them. Gradually more and more uses were found for the horse, and for each one new equipment was developed. During many centuries the horse was used as a means of transport, for hunting, and in war.

In the Middle Ages the saddle became something of a status symbol: a wealthy man would have three or four saddles, each for use on particular occasions. These saddles became family heirlooms and were handed down from generation to generation. In the United States many cowboys still carry on this tradition. They spend a lot of money on an expensive saddle which they then take everywhere with them, each putting his own saddle on any horse he is required to work. There is a great similarity between some saddles used years ago and those of today; the modern American cowboy saddle, for example, is very similar to the English saddle of the sixteenth century.

Riding today is primarily a pleasure sport. Throughout history horses were a vital means of transport; people rode out of necessity rather than for fun. Because of this, the pommel and cantle were developed to prevent the less good riders falling off. At that time, of course, there was no mechanical transport anywhere in the world: and if you had to choose between riding and walking, you rode, whether or not you were any good at it.

2 Basic equipment

The basic equipment needed for hacking and general riding for the
first-time horse owner is as follows: a well-fitting general purpose
saddle, a pair of stirrup leathers and irons, a girth, a snaffle bridle, a
headcollar, a grooming kit and tack cleaning equipment; perhaps

A leather-lined, general-purpose Saumur panel saddle, with stirrup irons and
leathers, a crupper and girths of string and webbing.

rugs and bandages. The list is not very daunting until you take yourself to a large saddlery shop and realise that the choice is enormous. I hope this book will help you to select the most suitable equipment for your own purposes, and to understand the principles upon which the variations have evolved.

The saddle

Choose a well-known make that is a suitable size for you and your horse or pony. It is important that neither the seat nor thigh length is too large for the rider, as it may cause him to slip backwards and out of the correct position. Before buying a saddle for yourself, sit in it (preferably on a horse), with an experienced horseman giving advice. Not all saddles are cut the same, and while one sixteen-inch saddle may have a short leg and a large seat, another may actually be for a rider with a long thigh and a small seat! So do get truly expert advice on this expensive purchase. A full-panel saddle,

How to put on a saddle correctly (photographs left and opposite):

The horse should be fitted with a headcollar and tied up in the stable. Attach the stirrup leathers and irons to the saddle and the girth to the right side. Place the numnah, if used, under the saddle. With the saddle in the crook of the left arm, approach the horse on the nearside, and pat him with your free hand to reassure him.

10

Place the saddle high up on the withers and slide it smoothly down into position.

Move under the horse's neck to reach the girth.

Let down the girth. Note the position of the saddle on the horse's spine.

Return to the horse's left side and do up the girth buckles.

though a little more expensive than the half-panel saddle, is well worth the extra cost as it is less likely to slip and is more comfortable. The best type of saddle at this stage of riding is a general-purpose one as it is designed to encourage the rider to sit correctly in the centre – the lowest part of the saddle. The general-purpose saddle is not exaggerated in design and allows the rider to sit correctly for basic dressage, elementary jumping and hacking; a deep and well-balanced seat should be achieved before you attempt to specialise in show-jumping, dressage, etc., where a particular style of saddle is required.

Stirrup leathers must be kept supple and in good condition and again it is worth buying the best you can afford. Particular attention should be given to the holes in the leather as these sometimes become stretched or enlarged with wear and will then be unsafe. The stitching must also be checked daily for signs of wear.

Two types of stirrup iron: the standard (left) and the safety, with its release catch.

Stirrup irons should always be made of stainless steel, never nickel. Metals other than stainless steel are too soft to be really safe: if the horse falls or the rider passes too close to a tree the iron may be crushed and serious damage occur to the horse or rider. Indeed, I have known a horse and rider slip and fall while riding cross-country: the nickel stirrup iron broke and caused a very severe injury to the horse's side. It is safer to pay more initially, and is also worth it in the long run as stainless steel irons will last a lifetime.

Girths There are four main types of girth: string, nylon, webbing and leather. The most common variations are described in more detail on pages 26 and 31–2.

Martingale

Predominantly used with jumpers, though they are also in general use. I have discussed these in more detail under show-jumping.

Bridle

The importance of careful fitting is as true for bridles as it is for saddles. An uncomfortable horse will never be relaxed and obedient, and an ill-fitting bridle will possibly make him head-shy

Parts of the bridle (from left to right):
headpiece, browband, cheekpieces, noseband, snaffle bit and reins.

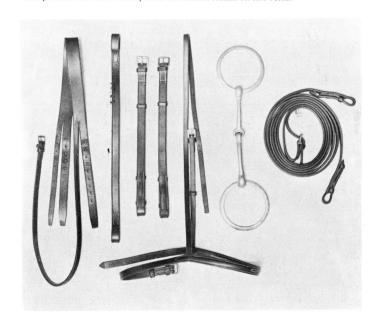

How to put on a bridle correctly:

Approach the horse on the nearside, slip the reins over his head and guide the bit into his mouth, using gentle pressure with the fingers to open the mouth. Your right hand holds the headpiece.

The headpiece can then be placed over the horse's ears.

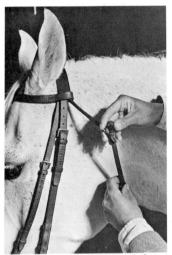 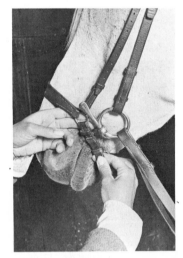

Do up the buckle of the throatlatch.

Fit the drop noseband and make sure that it is comfortable.

14

and give him a sore mouth into the bargain. When fitting a bridle here are some important points to watch:

1   The throatlatch should be as loose as possible to allow the horse to flex his jaw, without being so loose that the bridle could slip over his head. A clenched fist should fit between the throatlatch and the horse's throat and a hand between the cheek and the throatlatch.

2   The noseband should also be roomy. A good guide is to allow two fingers' breadth between the noseband and the horse's face. It should be fitted low enough to lie well below the horse's cheekbone.

3   The bit should be the correct width for the horse's mouth and must be fitted so that it just wrinkles the corners of the mouth. If it is too high or too low, it will hurt the mouth. The different types of bit and the principles behind them are discussed on pages 33–47.

Finally, pull the forelock over the browband. Notice the half spoon-cheek snaffle bit, fitted in an upward position to give a clear aid.

15

Headcollar

It is advisable to buy a strong headcollar and a stout, reasonably long, lead rope, rather than a halter with rope attached. Not only does the headcollar last longer, but you can leave it on your horse in the field if there is any possibility of his being difficult to catch. The headcollar should be adjusted so that it fits snugly but is not tight and uncomfortable. Remember, too, that headcollars need regular cleaning and soaping if they are to give you good service.

Grooming and tack cleaning kit

The standard grooming kit consists of: dandy brush, body brush and curry comb, water brush, hoof pick, mane and tail comb, two sponges, wisp, stable rubber – and a container in which to keep all these items so they do not get lost. The proper use of the grooming kit, and variations upon this basic kit, are described in *Stable Management Explained*, another title in this series. The kit needed for proper cleaning of tack is given below on page 51.

The basic essentials for a stabled riding horse: general-purpose saddle, stirrup leathers and irons, girth, snaffle bridle, headcollar and rope, rug and blanket and a grooming kit.

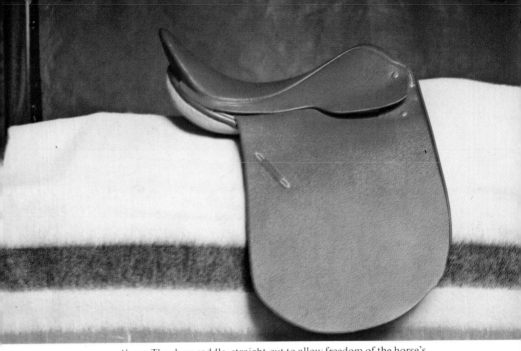

Above: The show saddle, straight-cut to allow freedom of the horse's shoulder and to display good conformation.

Below: The show-jumping saddle, forward-cut with a deep central seat. The suede knee roll gives added comfort for the rider.

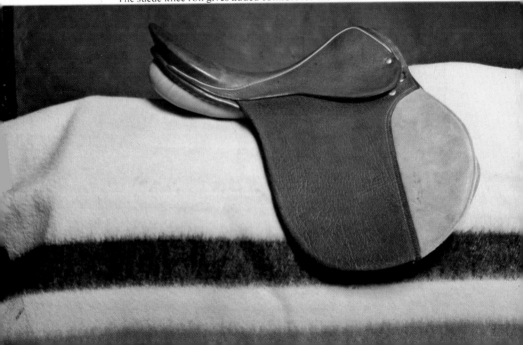

3 How the saddle is made

The best saddles are made to measure, as the best clothes are individually tailored. This is of course much more expensive than buying ready-made saddles and for most people is hardly practicable. It is interesting, however, to know how a top-quality saddle is designed and made to measure.

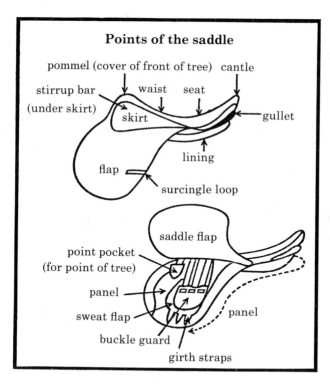

It is helpful to known the points of the saddle, and here you can see how the saddle is constructed.

The saddler will measure the horse by using a thin strip of soft lead which he places across the horse's back where the pommel or the saddle will be. He moulds the lead to the shape of the horse's back. The next step is for a drawing to be made of the lead mould, and it is from this drawing that the tree of the saddle is made. The tree is the foundation upon which the saddle is built. It used to be made of beechwood, strengthened with lightweight steel plates. Nowadays most trees are made of laminated wood; these are proving to be stronger, lighter and more durable. The tree must be sufficiently strong to stand up to galloping cross-country, hunting and jumping, and yet be light enough not to add an undue burden. Tree-making is a craftsman's job and there are fewer of these craftsmen than there once were. Some trees are now made, with reasonable success, with man-made materials; this type of saddle tends to be mass-produced, and while serving a useful purpose is not, in my opinion, as good as a hand-made saddle which has had a craftsman's care lavished on it.

When the saddler has a tree he can begin to make his saddle. First he will build a base on which to work. This is done by stretching webbing along the tree and then fitting a serge foundation. The tree is now covered, and the next task is to make the actual seat. As many of you will probably know, the seat is made of pigskin which is a very thin, exceptionally strong leather that will not stretch once fashioned to the required shape. The cutting of the leather and the making of the seat itself are highly skilled jobs, as it is essential that the seat is well fitted and has no trace of wrinkles. Next come the stirrup bars, which are made of steel and are attached to the tree. When firmly fitted they are covered with cowhide skirts which are sewn to the pigskin seat. The large saddle flaps, which are similar in shape to the skirt, are also cut and made from cowhide. Their actual shape varies depending on the type of saddle required. For example, a dressage or show saddle will have the flap cut rather straight to show off the horse's shoulder and give ample room for freedom of movement, while a jumping or racing saddle would need to have an exaggerated forward-cut flap to accommodate the rider's knee when short stirrups are being used for jumping or racing. The panels are also made in various styles depending on the type of saddle required. They are fitted to the head or front arch of the saddle, and should fit perfectly into the tree. It takes great skill on the part of the saddler to cut and shape the leather so that each piece is an exact fit.

The girth straps are fitted to the tree. It is more usual to have three girth straps than just the essential two; the third is there in case one of the others breaks. The girth straps take a tremendous strain, and have to be very strong and securely fitted. The saddle itself is finished by fitting guards to cover the girth buckles, which prevent the buckles from causing excessive wear on the underside of the flaps. The best girths are made of leather and will give years of service provided they are kept clean and supple; other types of girth (e.g. string, nylon or webbing) are also available.

A pair of stirrup leathers and irons completes the saddle. The leathers are made from tanned and cured leather, specially treated to give them extra strength. The tanning process, which transforms the skins of cattle, pigs and other animals into leather, is an interesting one. First the skins are cleaned and the hair removed, and then the skin is soaked in various solutions made from a base of tree bark. The leather is finally cured or finished, which removes the stretch from the leather and ensures a smooth and level surface.

4 Selecting your saddle

The types of saddle in general use nowadays are for the comfort of both horse and rider, to ensure that the rider is secure in the saddle and is able to achieve maximum results. The best type of saddle to use depends on the particular needs of the individual. If you are

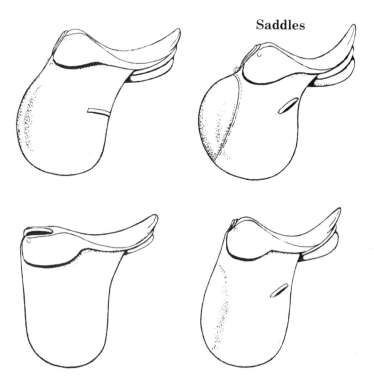

Saddles

Saddles in general use (from top left to right): all-purpose, jumping, show and dressage saddles.

just starting riding, then a general-purpose saddle is best. Show-jumping, eventing, dressage, showing, side-saddle and racing all have their own type of saddle, adapted for the different seat used in each kind of riding. Whichever type of saddle you require it must fit the horse. It is relatively easy to fit a saddle on a horse that is well-proportioned, with good conformation; the problem horses are those with high or flat withers or flat ribs, and over-fat ponies. Here are some points to observe when buying a saddle:

1   The saddle must be well balanced, which means that its weight is evenly distributed. There should be no undue pressure on the horse's loins or withers.

A well-fitting saddle viewed from the front; the front arch is balanced evenly and rests on the withers without pressure.

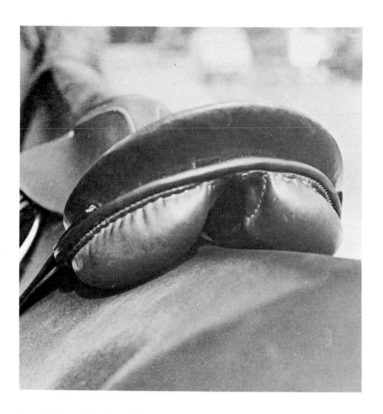

A well-fitting saddle viewed from behind; notice the clear channel along the horse's spine.

2   The front arch must be neither so narrow that it pinches the withers on either side, nor too wide as it will then press down on the withers.

3   The front panel must not restrict the movement of the shoulders.

4   There must be no pressure along the horse's spine. This is particularly important, as it is all too easy for a horse to acquire a pressure sore from an ill-fitting saddle. There should be a clear channel along the horse's spine when viewed from the rear, *when a rider is in the saddle.*

24

When a saddle is being fitted, ask someone to sit in the saddle. This will enable you to examine the fit as it will be in use. Very often saddles are bought and appear to fit the pony or horse without the rider, but as soon as the weight of the rider is on the saddle it no longer fits.

If you live in Britain and have a horse or pony for which you have difficulty in fitting a saddle, then I suggest that you go to a reputable saddler who is a member of the Worshipful Company of Master Saddlers and ask his advice. Many shops sell saddlery and riding wear, and these are all right for an experienced person, but it is better for the inexperienced to buy from a shop that displays the Master Saddlers' sign. You can be sure of finding an experienced person to fit the saddle for you, not just a sales assistant.

It is false economy to buy a cheap new saddle; a second-hand saddle by a well-known maker will hold its value and last for years, so try to find a good second-hand saddle rather than spending the same money on a new one of lesser quality. If you take proper care of the saddle it will give years of service. When the saddle is not in use it should be kept either on a saddle bracket attached to the wall or on a saddle horse, both of which are specially shaped to carry the saddle. The saddle horse is also used for cleaning tack.

The saddle should never rest on the ground for fear of damage to the tree or scratching of the leather work. If you do have to rest it on the ground for a moment, stand it up on the pommel rather than letting it lie spread-eagled on the ground. Never leave your horse tied up with his saddle on, as he may rub himself against a wall or fence and damage the saddle; he could even get down and roll, particularly if he has just been ridden and is hot and sweaty, and this could easily cause the tree of the saddle to be broken. When it is being carried, the saddle should be handled with just as much care. Carry it over your arm, with the front arch in the crook of the elbow. This leaves the other hand free to open doors, and to balance the saddle if it is very heavy.

The saddle may be lined with leather, linen or serge. Serge is not so commonly used nowadays as it is absorbent and very difficult to keep clean, and as a result does not last as long as linen or leather.

Leather is very long-lasting and easy to keep clean; however, it is rather cold and some very sensitive horses object to the cold on their backs and may be better with a linen-lined saddle, as are horses prone to saddle sores.

Types of girth

There are four main types of girth: leather, webbing, string and nylon; some in everyday use are listed here.

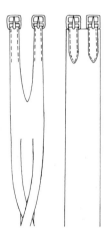

Two of the best types of girth, both made of leather: the Balding (above left) and Three Fold girths.

Three-Fold leather girth This is made of baghide leather and is usually hand-sewn. There are two rust-proof buckles at each end of the girth. Provided the girth is kept well oiled and supple it is very useful for hacking, schooling and general activities.

Leather Fitzwilliam girth This is another girth made of baghide. It is usually hand-sewn with six rust-proof buckles. The main girth is approximately 4in (10cm) wide and is three-fold leather. The overlay is made of bridle leather. This type of girth is ideal for hunting, jumping or polo.

A wire-ring German snaffle bridle, lightweight and mobile, useful for the novice horse.

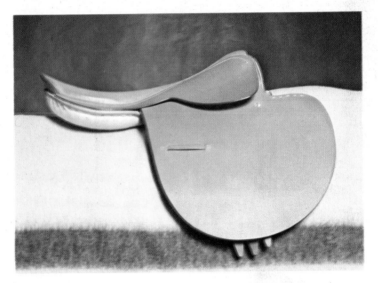

Above: The racing saddle, lightweight with cut-back head and forward-cut panel to make room for the jockey's knee.

Below: The dressage saddle, deep-seated in order to help the rider maintain a good, central seat.

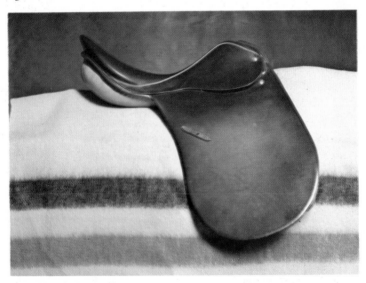

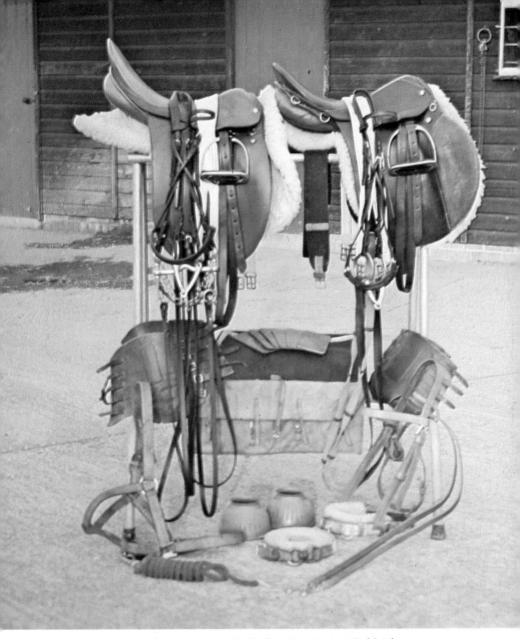

Equipment for eventing: dressage saddle (left) and jumping saddle (right), double and snaffle bridles, surcingle, numnahs, brushing and over-reach boots, lunge cavesson and rein, weight cloth and lead, leather headcollar and rope.

A snaffle bridle for showing in hand, with a coupling and lead rein
attached.

Humane girth This is yet another three-fold leather girth. It has self-adjusting 'humane' buckles which distribute girth pressure evenly.

Elastic end girth This girth is often used on hunters, eventers or as a race exercise girth. It is fitted with strong elastic at one end of the three-fold leather girth and allows the horse to breathe easily during exertion.

Anti-chafe girth This girth has become very popular as it permits easier breathing by a winded horse and automatically adjusts to fit, and the narrow shaping at the elbows helps to eliminate chafing. The girth has a reinforcing strip of strong cowhide stitched down the back, and may have double elastic at one end.

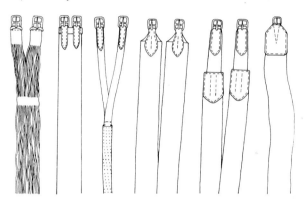

Types of girth (from left to right): nylon; Lampwick; tubular web; web; web with elastic insert; and all elastic.

Leather Balding or ribbon girth Another leather girth with four buckles, shaped to reduce chafing and galling as much as possible. It is often used on hunters and jumpers.

Tubular linen show girth This is the girth most commonly used for show saddles. It is made of white linen, the pimpled rubber lining

31

prevents the girth from slipping and the humane crossed-buckle arrangement ensures even distribution of girth pressure.

White cotton Fitzwilliam This is made of English cotton web and has a removable web lay. There are six buckles which are rust-proof.

Web girth This is a useful exercise, riding school or Pony Club camp girth as it is durable and inexpensive. The girth is made of strong, closely woven cotton web and has four buckles.

Nylon multi-strand girth This girth is made of super-strong woven nylon strands, and has four buckles. The girth is designed to help prevent chafing and the formation of sores. It washes easily and dries quickly.

5 Bits and bitting

There are basically four 'families' of bridle: the snaffle, the curb, the pelham and the bitless. All bridles give the rider control by operating on one or more points of the horse's head. These pressure points are the poll, the nose, the bars, corners and roof of the mouth, the tongue and the chin groove.

Bits are certainly influenced by changing fashions; you can buy numerous variations on the four different groups of bits. They are made from several different metals and materials − rubber, vulcanite, leather, nylon, stainless steel and the softer metals such as nickel. Let us look at each of the four groups in turn.

The snaffle

This is the mildest form of bit. The simplest is usually jointed, with two rounded bars linked in the middle, and has rings at each end. It acts on the corners of the mouth and its effect is to raise the horse's head. There are numerous varieties of snaffle. The seven main types are listed below, followed by examples of specific bits of the various types.

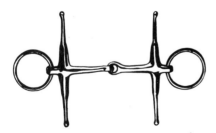

Australian loose-ring snaffle, sometimes known as the Fulmer snaffle. It was popularised in Britain by Mr Robert Hall. It is a mild bit with loose rings and long cheeks. It is extremely useful on young horses and is very kind and comfortable for the horse.

Rubber snaffle is also very mild and is made of Indiarubber with a chain passing through the centre. It is particularly useful for young horses or very sensitive animals that are light-mouthed and nervous of going on to the bit.

Eggbutt snaffle is a jointed bit with fixed rings, its advantages being that it minimizes the chances of pinching the lips, and is popular because it suits many horses. The mouthpiece is slightly thinner than that of the German snaffles and therefore the bearing surface is not so great. It is useful for hunting, jumping and dressage.

German snaffle is a lightweight bit with a hollow mouthpiece. It is thick in appearance and consequently allows a wider distribution of surface pressure. I like using this bit with young horses, and have found that most novice horses go kindly in it.

French bridoon or Gloucester snaffle has a double-jointed mouthpiece and is particularly useful on horses that are fussy in their mouths. It allows more mobility than the normal snaffle and is another useful bit for young horses.

Racing snaffle is a single-jointed snaffle and is thinner than the usual snaffle. It has 'dee' cheeks which help to prevent the bit from being pulled or sliding from one side to the other in the horse's mouth. As the mouthpiece is thin, the bearing surface is directed over a smaller area, and this bit is therefore a little stronger than the others previously mentioned.

Twisted snaffle is a strong bit and may have either loose rings or eggbutt rings. The centre piece has a single joint and the actual bit is twisted. It is severe in its action and is therefore used only on horses with very hard mouths. Personally it is not a bit that I have found very successful and I believe it was more fashionable immediately after the Second World War than it is today. It is, however, less severe than the double twisted wire snaffle which, though popular in many U.S. hunter and jumper stables, should be used only by experts and even then with caution.

Eggbutt mullen snaffle Made of vulcanite and fairly mild, this is a bit which allows plenty of room for the tongue.

Wire ring nylon mullen mouth snaffle The wire ring snaffles are particularly good on young horses as the large rings prevent the bit sliding through the horse's mouth and there is no risk of the lips being pinched.

Eggbutt mullen mouth snaffle Made of stainless steel, this bit allows room for the horse's tongue, but as the mouthpiece is a little thinner than the nylon version the bearing surface is not so great, and the bit is a little stronger.

Wire ring straight bar snaffle This bit operates on the tongue, the corners of the mouth and the bars. It is not suitable for young horses as they sometimes curl their tongues over the top of this type of bit.

Wire ring straight bar twisted snaffle This bit is very severe and is sometimes used on young entire horses when being handled; it is as a result also known as a straight bar stallion snaffle.

Eggbutt German snaffle This is a mild bit and is often used on young horses when schooling and in early dressage tests. The mouthpiece is thick, which allows for a wide bearing surface.

Wire ring jointed German snaffle This bit is not unlike the eggbutt

German snaffle, but the wire rings allow for a little more mobility in the bit than the eggbutt snaffle.

Jointed slotted eggbutt snaffle This snaffle again operates on the corners of the mouth; the cheek pieces pass through each slot and hold the bit in position.

Flat-ring jointed snaffle or plain snaffle This type of bit is often used for exercising hunters on non-hunting days. Its disadvantage is that the hole which the flat ring passes through becomes worn over a period of time and may pinch the corners of the mouth.

Half spoon-cheek snaffle Particularly useful on jumping horses to help keep them straight.

Half spoon-cheek snaffle bridle with the half spoon at the top. This position helps in giving a clear aid to a young horse.

A double bridle, fitted with wire-ring bridoon and a Weymouth curb bit,
used in advanced dressage competitions.

Plain cheek snaffle or ball cheek snaffle Useful on young horses whose mouths are not really made; the long cheeks assist with turning and prevent the bit sliding through the horse's mouth.

Full spoon-cheek snaffle Not very different from the loose ring spoon-cheek snaffle, this bit operates directly on the corners of the mouth, tongue and bars, whereas there is more mobility in the loose-ring bit.

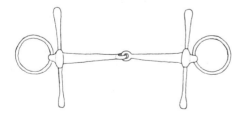

Loose ring spoon-cheek snaffle A fairly mild bit; the spoon cheeks help to keep the horse straight and it is particularly useful when jumping a green or novice horse.

The pelham

This is a variation of the curb bit and tries to combine the snaffle and curb as one bit. It operates on the bars of the mouth and, with a curb chain, on the chin groove. A pelham is often used on children's ponies that are a little too strong for them. It may be used with two reins or with 'roundings', a piece of leather attached to the two rein rings, to which the single rein is attached. I feel that with one rein only the bit becomes contradictory as it cannot operate on the chin groove and the corners of the mouth at the same time. With two reins one can have the curb pressure by taking the bottom rein and the same action as a snaffle by taking the top rein; if you use both reins simultaneously you lose the subtlety and sensitivity of the bit. Nevertheless, many ponies seem to go well in this bit even when only one rein is used. Here are some examples of different types of pelham bits.

Arch-mouth pelham bit A lightweight bit which is kind to sensitive-mouthed horses as the bit is fairly thick and mullen mouthed, allowing plenty of room for the tongue.

42

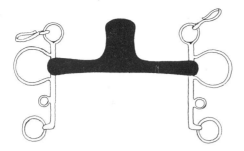

Port mouthed pelham bit This is used when the horse tends to grip the bit. It is more severe than the previous pelham as it operates on the roof of the mouth as well as the corners and tongue.

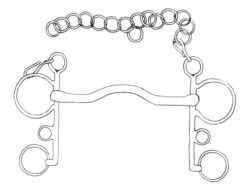

Hartwell pelham bit A heavyweight bit with a curved ported mouth; used when a more severe bit is required.

Half-moon or mullen mouth pelham bit A very popular and easy bit for horse and rider. The straight bar is excellent for soft-mouthed horses. This type of pelham is used with two reins or with roundings.

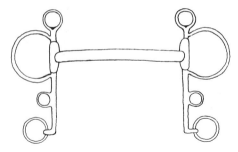

Eggbutt pelham bit A comfortable bit for the horse as the eggbutt cheeks eliminate pinching.

Flexible rubber mouth pelham A mild bit often used in the hunting field.

The jointed pelham It has the normal cheek and curb action with

44

the jointed mouthpiece, thus trying to create a nutcracker action and endeavouring to do the job of curb and snaffle.

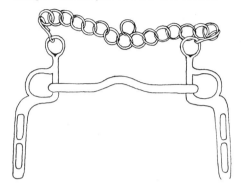

Army pelham bit A slight port mouth gives this bit a little more control over very strong horses.

The Scamperdale It was invented by the late Sam Marsh and is to my mind one of the most useful pelhams. It overcomes the problems of chafing by having the mouthpiece turned back at each end.

The kimblewick or Spanish jumping bit It is a popular bit with children's ponies. Its action is the same as that of other pelhams, but is somewhat shorter in its cheeks and by its shape allows the

rein to slip to the bottom of the cheeks when a rider carries his hands low, thus giving more poll and curb pressure. It is not a bit that I would recommend to be used all the time, but it is a good 'change' bit for variety and effect. It is perhaps best used when strong ponies are actually being jumped, an ordinary snaffle being used the rest of the time.

The double bridle

The double consists of two bits; the bridoon or snaffle, and the curb bit. The bridoon, like the ordinary snaffle, raises the horse's head and puts pressure on the corners of the mouth and on the tongue; the curb encourages the horse to lower his head and flex his jaw and operates on the bars and roof of the mouth, on the poll and the chin groove. The combined effect allows the rider to have more delicate and refined control over a well-trained horse, as is required for showing or dressage. This bit should never be used by an inexperienced rider or on an inexperienced horse. There are two main kinds of curb bits: the Banbury and the Weymouth. The

The Banbury curb bit showing how the cheeks enable the mouthpiece to revolve.

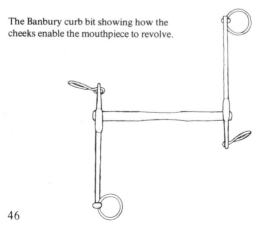

Banbury has a straight mouthpiece tapered at the centre. It operates not only on the bars, lips and chin groove but also on the roof of the mouth. It is slightly more severe than the more popular Weymouth, which has either a sliding or a fixed mouthpiece and either a tongue groove or a port in the centre of the mouthpiece which allows the tongue to lie comfortably: otherwise the action is the same as other curb bits.

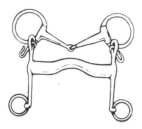

Dressage Weymouth bit and eggbutt bridoon.

Loose-cheek Weymouth bit and bridoon with double link curb chain.

The bitless bridle

There are two main types: the scawbrig and the hackamore. The first is a very simple arrangement, asserting pressure on the nose and a little into the chin groove. The hackamore is slightly more complicated in its design, though the principle is the same as the scawbrig as pressure is asserted on the nose and the chin groove. I personally find the scawbrig a very useful bridle for a horse with

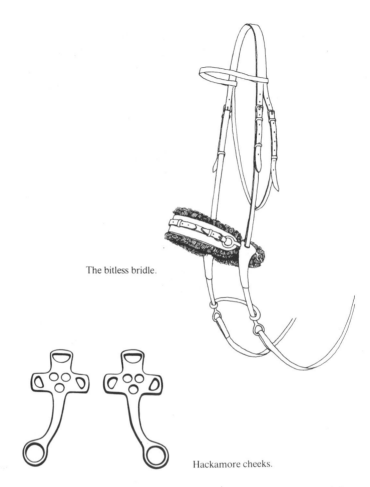

The bitless bridle.

Hackamore cheeks.

some mouth trouble. The hackamore is a little stronger and has been used with great success on show-jumpers; see also Western riding, pages 89–90.

Bit parts

The curb chain is a chain with small, flat links, usually seventeen of them, which fits into the chin groove and is attached to the curb bit by a special hook. It is kept in position by the lip strap, a rounded strip of leather which is fitted onto the 'dees' on the bit and passes through the flylink on the curb chain. (The flylink is a separate single link in the centre of the curb chain.) There are many types of curb chain; here are some of them.

Leather curb chains These are made of bridle leather, lined and stitched, with non-rust chain ends. This is a very mild type of curb chain.

Rubber curb chain guards These are made of pure gum rubber and slide over the curb chain to ensure that the curb chain is comfortable for the horse.

Double link curb chain A little more severe than the leather curb chain, but the double links ensure a long-lasting chain and it is very widely used with great success.

Flat circle link chain This chain is used without a rubber guard and is most severe, as the circular links can sometimes cause pinching to the chin groove. If used with a rubber guard, however, it becomes as mild as the leather curb chain, with the added advantage that the chain will last longer than the leather one.

49

6 Care and cleaning of saddlery

Tack or saddlery is expensive, and should always be kept in good repair, clean and supple. It is essential to inspect your tack every day so that weaknesses in the stitching or leather are noticed immediately; pay extra special attention to girth stitching and buckles. The leather must be fed with oil or fat or it will dry out and crack – olive oil, glycerine and castor oil are all excellent for keeping the leather soft. When buying saddle soap check the glycerine content: if it is high, the saddle soap will be of good quality and will help to keep the leather pliable.

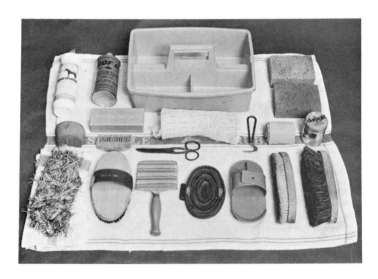

A kit for grooming and for cleaning tack. *From top left, back row:* Horse shampoo, hoof oil, kit box, two sponges. *Centre row:* Sponge and saddle soap, mane comb, scissors, cactus cloth, hoof pick, tail bandage and metal polish. *Front row:* Wisp on stable rubber, body brush, metal, plastic and rubber curry combs, water brush and dandy brush.

If your saddlery is out of use for a long time it should be stored in a warm, dry place. It is best to go over all the leather with vaseline, kochalin or neatsfoot oil, which will keep the leather pliable while it is in store.

Cleaning tack

Your saddlery should be cleaned every time it has been used in order to keep it in really good condition. The actual cleaning task will then be simple, as the tack will never be excessively dirty.

Equipment necessary for cleaning tack

1 A saddle horse
2 An anchor (a hook to hang bridles on)
3 Bucket of warm water
4 A piece of old towelling, very good for washing leather
5 A sponge for saddle soap
6 A chamois leather for drying
7 A bar of glycerine saddle soap
8 A dandy brush for removing mud and sweat from the underside of linen or serge saddles
9 Metal polish
10 Cloth to apply metal polish, and duster to remove it and give shine

Procedure for cleaning a saddle

1 Put the saddle on the saddle horse.
2 Remove the girth, stirrup leathers and stirrup irons.
3 Cleaning the underside of the saddle first, wash the whole of a leather saddle with the towelling cloth wrung out in water; saddles lined with linen or serge may have their undersides brushed with a dandy brush.
4 Dry all the leather with a chamois leather.
5 With a damp sponge and saddle soap go over all the leather with the saddle soap, rubbing it well in and paying equal

Saddle stripped for cleaning, with Balding girth and stirrup leathers on the saddle horse. Stirrup irons, saddle soap and sponges are on the shelf below. All pieces need to be washed thoroughly before polishing.

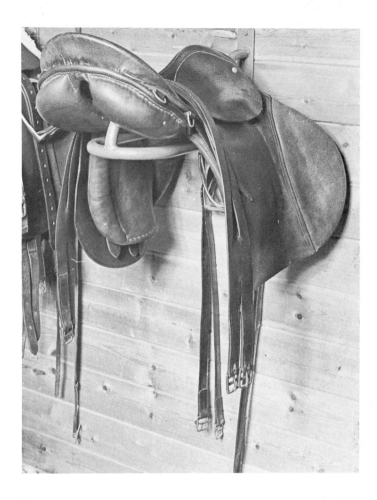

The saddle cleaned and put up correctly, with its stirrup irons and leathers detached for storage.

attention to both sides of flaps, etc. Do not let the sponge become too damp or the soap will lather and smear.

6   Wash stirrup leathers and leather girth, and dry with chamois leather. Webbing, string and nylon girths may be washed too, not after each use, but frequently.

7   Go over girth and stirrup leathers thoroughly with saddle-soaped sponge.
8   Polish stirrup irons and shine with duster.
9   Put saddle up on saddle rack and reassemble, laying the girth tidily over the top of the saddle.

Procedure for cleaning a bridle

1   Undo all buckles and take bridle to pieces.
2   Wash and dry the bit; polish cheekpiece, but never the mouthpiece (*you* taste it!), with metal polish and cloth.
3   Wash all leather work with damp cloth, dry with chamois and saddle soap with sponge and soap.
4   Put bridle together and hang on peg.
5   Attach bit.
6   'Put up' by passing reins through throatlatch for neatness, and fastening noseband loosely round outside of the rest of the bridle.

7 Training equipment

Initially the equipment for training is the same as for normal exercising: the horse will require a bridle and a saddle with girth, stirrup irons and leathers. In addition, brushing boots, lungeing cavesson, lungeing rein, lungeing whip, lungeing roller, side reins, driving or long reins and gloves for the trainer will be required.

Details of how to use this equipment are given in *Training Explained*, also in this series.

Brushing boots: On the left, hind boots of leather and kersey; on the right, two polo boots of felt and leather.

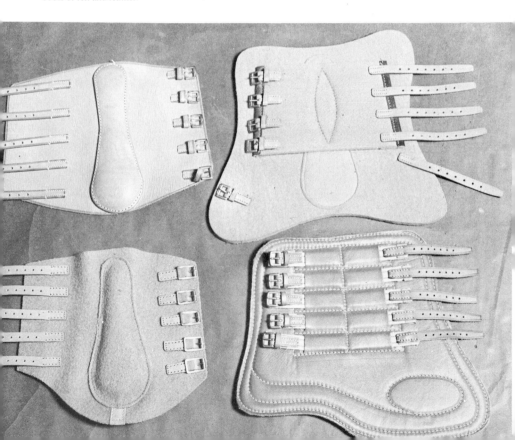

Brushing boots

These are a protective covering of felt, leather or vinyl wrapped around the lower leg, held in position by leather, velcro or elastic straps, which protect the horse's legs should he knock them by brushing one leg against another (see photograph on previous page).

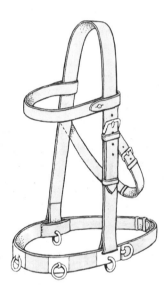

A lightweight lungeing cavesson. Notice the swivel rings which prevent the lunge line from becoming twisted.

Lungeing cavesson

It should be of strong leather, have a centre ring which swivels and fit snugly. The swivel rings will prevent the lunge line becoming twisted.

Long reins or driving reins

These should be 25ft (7.6m) in length and be made of lightweight webbing. The first 8ft (2.5m) from the bit should be rolled leather

This horse is being lunged over small jumps on a long rein attached to a lungeing cavesson.

Dressed for lungeing: bridle, brushing and over-reach boots, roller, lungeing cavesson and rein, side reins; and lunge whip in the trainer's hand.

or $^1/_2$-in (12mm) rope, which allows the rein to slip easily through the 'dee' rings or terrets of the lunge roller.

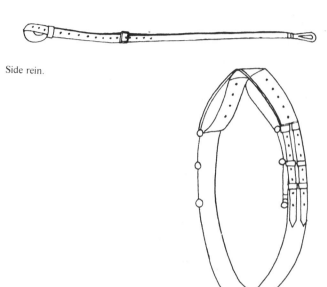

Side rein.

Lunge roller.

Side reins

There are two main types: plain leather, and leather with an insert of rubber or elastic. Reins with rubber or elastic inserts are preferable as they have a little more 'give'. In the United States side reins are often made of nylon material rather than leather.

Plain side reins These must be adjustable, with spring clips to attach them from the roller to the cavesson or the bit rings. Plain reins ensure a constant pressure of contact with the horse at all times.

Elastic or rubber side reins In principle these are a good idea as they allow a little more give than the plain side reins. Unfortunately it is often the case that the elastic insert is rather old and consequently the side rein becomes too slack and does not allow a constant contact. Some modern elastic side reins have leather behind the elastic so that the elastic can only stretch to the length of the leather support. This is to my mind a more satisfactory arrangement.

Lunge roller

This must be well padded so there is no unnecessary pressure on the horse's spine, and must be kept supple. The most suitable type for training will have three rings on each side to enable you to vary the height of the side reins according to individual needs.

Gloves

The rider/trainer should always wear gloves for lungeing or long reining as well as riding. In training a horse it may pull hard at you and badly burn your hands through the friction of the webbing, rope or leather. Leather or string gloves are best.

8 Show-jumping equipment

The saddle

There are various types and designs of saddle on the market, adapted for the different seat used in each kind of riding. The jumping saddle is designed to bring the rider's weight well forward. There are many designs of jumping saddle suited for show-jumping. The weight of the saddle you choose will depend on your size and actual requirements, but you should look for one that is well-balanced, with a deep central seat and forward-cut, perhaps with a knee roll. The bars for the stirrup leathers are positioned more forward than on other saddles and should be recessed for leg comfort.

The Cavalier is a forward-cut, lightweight saddle with low girth straps and an all-in-one panel which allows the rider to feel very close to the horse. The low girth straps make the saddle particularly comfortable as the buckles of the girth are not in a position where they may interfere with the rider's leg. As there are only two girth straps on this saddle and the fitting of the girth is difficult when mounted, it is important when competing in jumping competitions to use a surcingle, or what the Americans call an 'overgirth', on top of the saddle for added security. I personally find these saddles beautifully comfortable for both horse and rider and they really help the rider to maintain a good jumping position.

The forward-cut jumping saddle with normal girth straps also allows plenty of room for the rider's knee and thigh to be forward in front of him, giving greater security and balance. Some saddles have suede knee rolls for added comfort when the rider's weight needs to be well forward, as when show-jumping. In the United States the 'close contact' jumping saddle, which has no knee-roll, is becoming more popular.

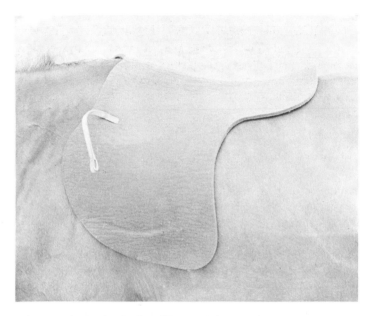

A felt numnah, placed under the saddle to stop it from rubbing the horse's spine.

Numnah

This is a pad which is shaped to the size of the saddle. It can be made of sheepskin or of man-made fibre. A saddle must fit the horse without a numnah, although a numnah can serve as a temporary measure if the saddle is due for re-stuffing. When show-jumping the horse will use the whole of his body to maximum extent, jumping with a round back, so for this reason, a thick numnah will be necessary; otherwise when the horse makes a 'bascule' over the fence his spine may touch the central channel of the saddle, causing him to lose concentration and perhaps knock a fence down. When fitting a numnah care must be taken to ensure that the centre front of the numnah is lifted up into the arch of the saddle so as to avoid putting unnecessary pressure on the horse's withers. The numnah should be sufficiently large to be seen about $1\frac{1}{2}$in (3.5cm) below the edge of the saddle.

Man-made numnahs are easy to look after as they may be washed by hand in warm water and left to dry, or washed in a machine. Sheepskin ones are more of a problem; they are best brushed very well every day and from time to time washed by hand with a mild soap and dried naturally in the air. Do not put them in a washing machine.

This double-sided nylon numnah provides good protection when jumping and is easy to keep clean.

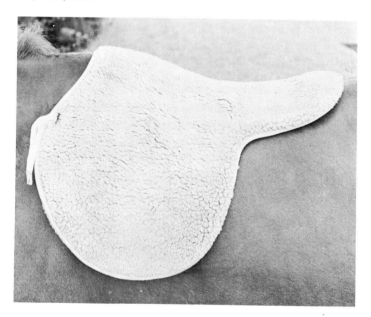

Bridles

A snaffle, double bridle or pelham may be used. If your horse goes well in a simple snaffle bridle, this is of course preferable.

Martingales

In addition to the horse's usual bridle it may be necessary for the show-jumper to wear a martingale. The purpose of the martingale is to assist in the control of the horse's head and neck, enabling him to see the fence and be well balanced in the approach stride. There are several different types of martingale.

Running martingale This type is most commonly used for jumping competitions. Its purpose is to regulate and control the horse's head in the approach to a fence, while allowing freedom of the head and neck in flight as the rider's hands follow the movement of the horse's head down and forward. The martingale is attached to the girth between the horse's forelegs. The neckstrap is fitted so as to hold the leather strap from the girth in position. The end of the martingale divides into two straps with a ring on each strap, through which the rein passes. The running martingale achieves its effect by applying pressure to the horse's mouth.

A running martingale should be used with 'stops', small pieces of rubber or leather attached to the rein near the bit end to prevent the ring of the martingale catching on the ring of the bit or hooking over the rein buckles.

Fitting a running martingale (see opposite, overleaf and page 71)

1 Place the loop of the neckstrap over the horse's head.
2 Pass the girth through the loop of the martingale.
3 Take the opposite end of the martingale with both rings in one hand and lie it up the horse's shoulder. The rings should not quite reach the withers. A good guide is to leave a hand's width between the withers and the rings.
4 Unbuckle reins. Pass each rein through the martingale rings.
5 Note the stops that prevent the rings from slipping over the rein attachments.
6 From the ground take up the rein contact as though you were mounted; the martingale should be at a length to prevent the horse carrying his head too high. If too long, adjust by shortening another hole or so.

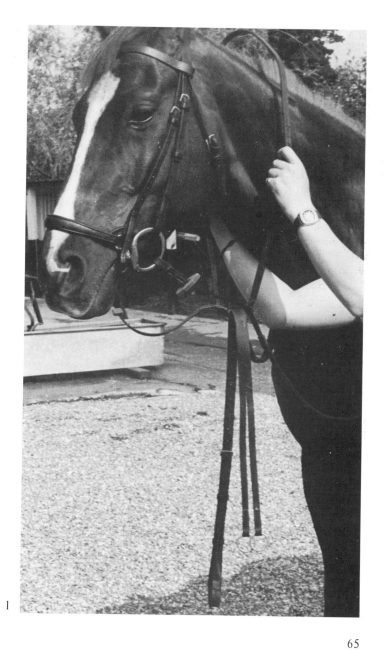

1

2

3

4

5

66

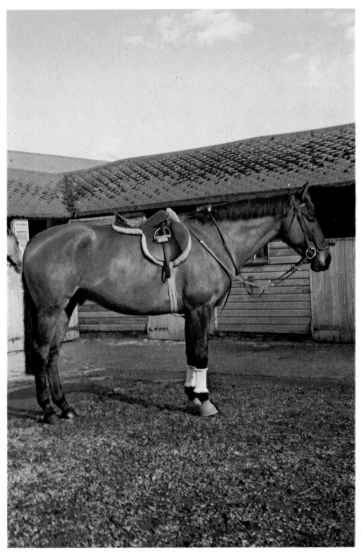

Dressed for jumping: forward-cut saddle, sheepskin numnah, running martingale, eggbutt snaffle bridle and drop noseband, exercise bandages and over-reach boots. It would be safer to fasten a surcingle over the saddle.

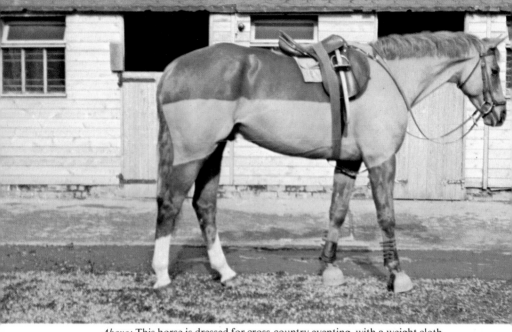

Above: This horse is dressed for cross-country eventing, with a weight cloth under the forward-cut jumping saddle.

Below: Dressed for road exercise on a cold day with a quarter sheet worn beneath the general-purpose saddle, and kneecaps for protection against a fall.

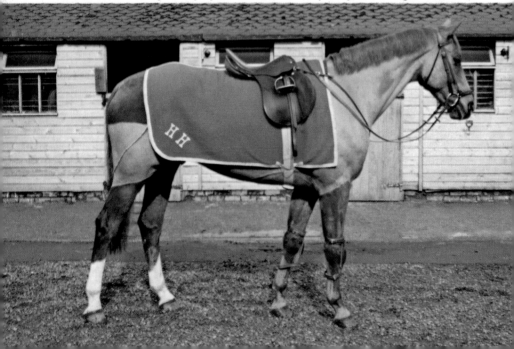

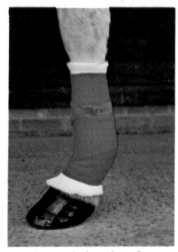

Above: Exercise bandage used to give extra support to the horse's tendons, and (above right) stable bandage with gamgee, for warmth.

Below: A New Zealand rug, waterproof and lined with wool, fastened with leg straps as well as a roller.

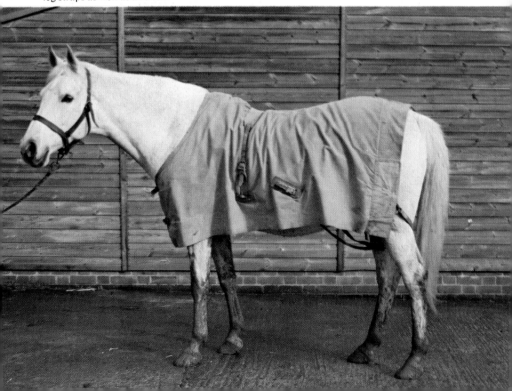

Dressed for the cross-country phase of a one-day event. Notice the surcingle fitted over the saddle for security. Over-reach boots and brushing boots are also fitted.

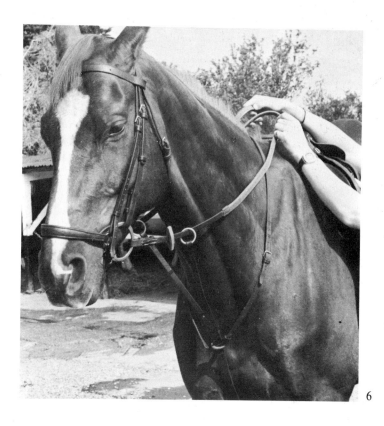

6

Standing martingale This is a leather strap attached from the girth to a cavesson noseband. It must never be attached to a drop noseband as this is too severe and would restrict the horse's breathing. The strap from the girth to the cavesson is supported by a neckstrap, as in the running martingale. The purpose of the standing martingale is to prevent the horse getting his head above the usual angle of control, thus ensuring that his head is in the best position in the approach to a fence. It achieves its effect by applying pressure to the horse's nose. It is the most popular martingale in the United States, although it may not be used in show-jumping competitions governed by international rules.

Fitting a standing martingale (see below, opposite and overleaf)

1 Place the neckstrap over the horse's head with the buckle end of the long strap nearest the forelegs.
2 Pass the girth through the loop of the buckle end of the martingale.
3 Attach the opposite end of the martingale strap to the cavesson noseband.
4 With the horse standing with head in correct position, place a hand underneath the leather strap and push towards the horse's gullet. It should just reach into the gullet when correctly adjusted.

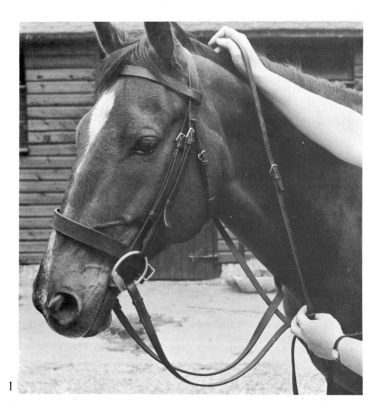

1

2

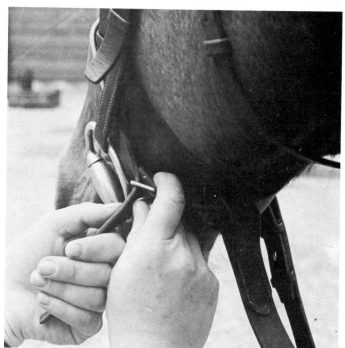

3

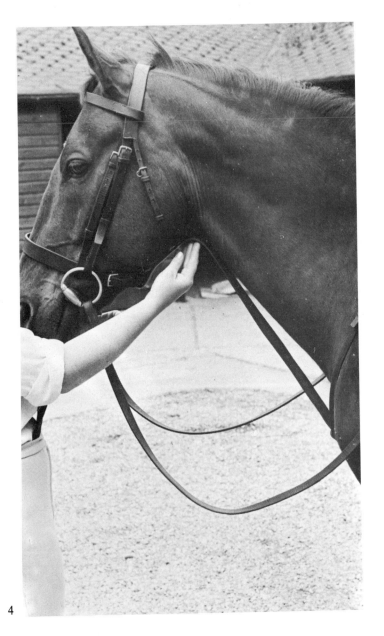

4

Irish martingale This type is used in racing and is useful if the horse tosses his head too much, when the rider might lose both reins over the horse's head. The Irish martingale is a piece of leather, about $1\frac{1}{2}$ in (3.5cm) wide and 6in (15cm) long, with a ring at each end. The martingale is fitted by passing the reins underneath the horse's neck through each ring. I have found it helpful on an impetuous show-jumper which does not require either the standing or the running martingale.

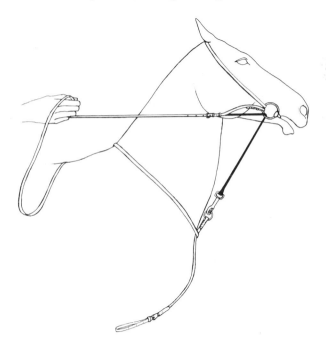

Here the horse's head is up and the straps have tightened. The Market Harborough is useful on a headstrong horse.

Market Harborough

This type of martingale is sometimes used on very strong horses when show-jumping. It should not be used by an inexperienced rider. At the girth end it is the same as the other martingales, with a loop for the girth to pass through and a ring at the chest. It is supported by a neckstrap in the same way as running and standing martingales. Attached to the ring at the chest are two straps which pass in an upwards direction through the rings of the bit. They are fastened to the ordinary rein by an adjusting snap hook or buckle, which is then fastened to one of the four metal 'dees' which are sewn on the reins. The Market Harborough only comes into effect when the horse's head is raised too high; in flight over a fence it allows complete freedom of the head and neck.

Over-reach or bell boots (top): leather with buckles, or rubber pull-on boots. In the centre, a lower brushing fetlock boot for the horse that strikes himself low down when jumping. The over-reach boot (below) fits round the fetlock.

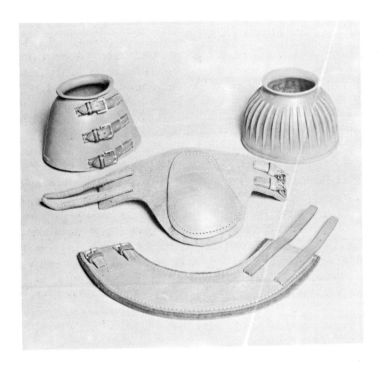

76

Boots

Boots are an essential part of the show-jumper's equipment; these are the most important types.

Over-reach boots A horse will often over-reach after jumping a big fence. This is when he lands unbalanced and the toe of the hind shoe strikes the heel of the forefoot. There are various designs of over-reach boots. Basically they should fit closely round the pastern and are shaped like a bell — American readers will know them as 'bell boots'. Some boots are the pull-on variety made of rubber. Others are made of leather, felt or PVC, and buckle or clip on to make fitting easy. Personally I prefer rubber over-reach boots that pull on, as although they are hard on finger-nails they are certainly more secure and safe. An unsafe boot could cause a horse to come down when jumping and the buckle may interfere with the horse's action.

Brushing boots The show-jumper will need these to protect his legs from injury should he knock fences when jumping. Some horses also move rather closely in front or behind, which will cause them to knock one fetlock with the opposite hoof and the boots will prevent injury from these knocks. There are many types of brushing boots available. *Felt shin and ankle boots or brushing boots* are made of felt with a heavy leather cap for protection against hitting. Front boots usually have three adjustable elastic straps and buckles for secure fitting, while the hind boots have four or five straps. *Kersey galloping or brushing boots* are mainly used when schooling the show-jumper. They are made of fine grey wool — kersey — and give well-padded protection. *Leather boots* are similar in design to the kersey and felt boots, but are made of fine leather. It is important to keep them soft and supple to avoid rubbing the horse sore in the fetlock area. Leather boots are very hard-wearing and in general will last longer than kersey or felt if you take the trouble to keep them clean and well soaped. *Vinyl brushing boots* with nylon or fleece backing and velcro or elastic fastenings are also popular nowadays.

9 Dressage equipment

The equipment required for dressage is relatively simple compared with that required for the show-jumper.

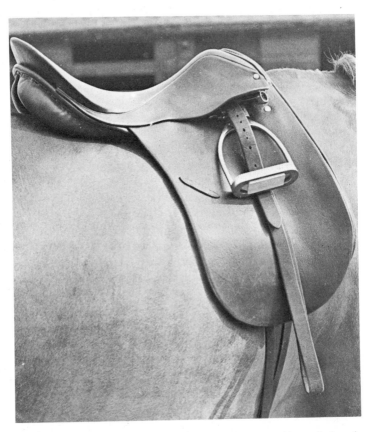

A well-fitting dressage saddle, viewed from the side. Note its position on the horse's spine.

Dressed for travelling home after an event: sweat rug under a woollen day rug, tail guard, kneecaps and stable bandage.

Above: Equipment for travelling. The day rug is quartered back to allow air to circulate on a mild day, and hock boots as well as kneecaps are fitted.

Below: The anti-sweat rug. When used in the stable, this needs a roller to prevent the rug from slipping.

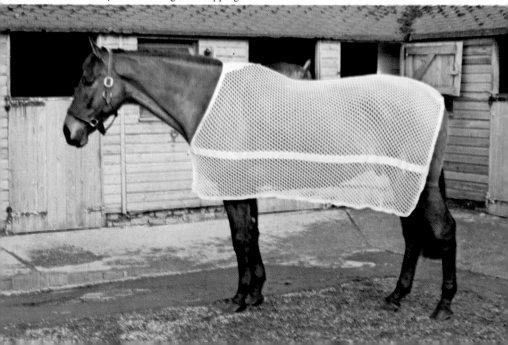

The saddle

The saddle used should be shaped to encourage the rider to sit in its central and lowest part. A full-panel model is best as there is less chance of the saddle slipping. Dressage saddles are cut fairly straight as the rider will have a longer leg position than the show-jumper's short forward style. The fitting of the saddle is particularly important as a badly fitting saddle may be the reason for the horse not being able to give his best. The weight of the saddle must be evenly distributed over the lumbar muscles, leaving the loins free.

From time to time it will be necessary for the saddle to be re-stuffed, because constant wear will cause the padding to become thin and the saddle will press down on the horse and possibly make him sore. It is a sensible precaution to have the saddle re-stuffed and the stitching checked once a year.

The bridle

An ordinary snaffle bridle is used in preliminary and novice tests; for elementary tests and those at more advanced levels a simple double bridle may be used. Artificial aids such as martingales and bearing, side or running reins are all forbidden, as are over-reach boots and bandages. In international dressage competitions a double bridle is always worn.

10 Equipment for horse trials

The tack that the horse will need for horse trials, also known as eventing, is fairly extensive as the event horse is required to do dressage, show-jumping and cross-country.

The bridle

A *snaffle bridle* will be needed for exercising, and in novice events for the dressage phase. The *double bridle* is only necessary on the advanced dressage horse where greater accuracy and precision is required.

The saddle

The dressage saddle is for the first phase of the event only, and should assist the rider in maintaining the best possible position in the saddle in order that maximum marks are achieved for this phase. For the other phases a jumping saddle, fulfilling the same requirements as those for the show-jumpers, will be needed. The saddle must fit well and be forward cut with good knee rolls to enable the rider to be secure and in good balance at all times.

It is advisable to fit a surcingle over the saddle to ensure that the saddle stays in exactly the right position; it is also a wise precaution in the event of a girth strap breaking or coming undone. Three numnahs will be needed, one for each phase of the event. It is not advisable to try to use the same one through every phase, as the horse is bound to sweat and a wet numnah will give him a sore back.

Protective equipment

Boots or bandages in front and behind will protect the horse

82

from knocks or bangs when galloping across country and also from knocking one leg against the other.

Over-reach boots are an equally important part of the horse's equipment, as it is likely that he may cut himself should he become unbalanced on landing after a fence. These boots will protect the horse's heels.

Lungeing equipment

A cavesson, lunge line and whip are necessary when schooling the horse, and lungeing is also an excellent way of working the horse, without having to put a rider on his back. This is an ideal way of warming up a fresh horse before the dressage phase of an event. A fuller explanation of how to lunge may be found in *Training Explained*.

Weight

In all two and three day events, also in advanced one day events, the rider must weigh 11st 11lb (in the United States the required weight for all events in the preliminary division or above is 165lb). A small person may need a heavier saddle or to carry weights to help make up the weight. Weights can be carried in a cloth fitted under the saddle; some eventing saddles have weight pockets on the saddle itself.

11 Equipment for hunting and hunter trials

The saddlery used for hunting and hunter trials must be comfortable for both horse and rider and, above all, be strong. The stitching must be checked regularly, the leather work kept clean and supple.

The saddle

The best type to use for hunting and hunter trials is a modern general-purpose saddle. It will not be necessary for the saddle to be as straight-cut as the dressage saddle, neither will it need to be as exaggeratedly forward-cut as the show-jumper's saddle. It must, though, be strongly built and comfortable for both horse and rider.

The bridle

In hunting and hunter trials this may be a double or a snaffle bridle, depending on the horse's level of training. It is best that the novice horse wear a snaffle bridle. The hunting snaffle bridle should be made from good leather and have no fancy stitching. The reins should be laced leather or rubber-covered, both of which prevent the rider's hands from slipping when the horse is wet with rain or sweat. Hunting breastplates with martingale attachment are often used on hunters and jumpers to control the horse's head and to keep the saddle in the correct position.

12 Equipment for show classes

The show horse needs a general-purpose saddle and snaffle bridle for exercising and everyday use, but when competing it will need special tack.

The saddle

A style that is straight cut shows the front of the horse to its best advantage. A popular saddle in use today is the Lane-Fox show saddle. This excellent saddle has a full cut-back head, is well proportioned with straight-cut flaps to show the horse's conformation to perfection, and the safety bars are recessed to eliminate any bulk at the knee. These saddles are usually sewn by hand, the saddler using a tree made of beechwood.

There are many different makes and designs of show saddle available but the essential points to remember are these:

1   The saddle must be straight cut to show the horse's shoulders to best advantage.
2   It must fit the horse perfectly without a numnah.
3   It must be comfortable for both competitor and judge.

Straight-cut show saddle.

In the United States cutback show saddles, known as 'park' or 'saddle seat' saddles are used primarily on such breeds as the American Saddlebred, Morgan and Arabian. Their design and fit should allow totally free movement of the horse's shoulder and not interfere with the naturally high head carriage of these breeds.

The bridle

In novice showing, hack or riding horse classes it is usual to produce the horse in a snaffle bridle: the ideal bridle will be of best quality leather and workmanship. It is all hand-sewn and is rounded wherever possible. The bridle will have hook-in stud fastenings and be easy to adjust to fit various horse's heads. The browband and cavesson noseband are rounded. The reins will also be of rounded leather, being $^3/_4$-in (18mm) at the hand. No coloured browbands, please.

Novice hunters are sometimes shown in lightweight snaffle bridles. This too should be hand-sewn and light, to show off the horse's head to advantage. As soon as they have progressed beyond the early stages, show hacks, hunters, cobs and ponies should all be shown in a double bridle. Ponies and show hacks should wear a hand-sewn rounded double bridle with a Weymouth curb bit; hunters and cobs should wear a plain leather double bridle.

13 Racing equipment

The saddle

Of a special lightweight design with cut-back head and forward-cut panel to accommodate the jockey's short leg position. The girth normally used is an elastic end girth, as this allows the horse to breathe easily during exertion.

Forward-cut racing saddle.

A surcingle is always used in addition to the girth. This is an additional safety device to ensure that the saddle stays in position should by any chance the girth break or the saddle slip.

Stirrup irons are mainly made of lightweight steel.

Stirrup leathers are usually made of rawhide, which is so strong as to be almost unbreakable. The jockey's stirrup leathers have to take considerable strain, so it is essential that they are very strong.

A number cloth

This is worn under the saddle so that when horses are moving at speed it is easy to identify each one; *the weight cloth* is also fitted under the saddle.

Blinkers or hoods

These are used for a horse who may look back, perhaps be worried at the start of a race or who does not jump straight.

14 Western equipment

Western bits

There are two main types of Western bit.

Loose jaw curb bit This bit has a solid copper mouthpiece which prevents dryness and increases the flow of saliva. The cheeks are made of steel and are chrome-plated. The design is intended to eliminate pinching.

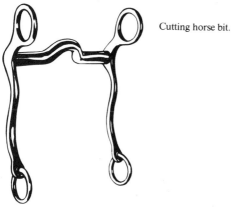

Cutting horse bit.

Cutting horse bit This bit is best with a straight shank rather than the swept-back style: the straightness allows for quicker response. The mouth-piece does not have a cut-back tongue groove as you do not want the cutting horse's head to come up.

Hackamores

A hackamore is a bitless bridle controlling the horse mainly by poll, nose and chin groove pressure. Here are some different types.

The hellymore This is a great favourite with Western riders. It has 8-in (20cm) cheeks with curb strap loops. The noseband is covered in leather and is self-adjusting. The pivot headstall pieces prevent the hackamore from tipping forward. It is excellent for training or for all-purpose riding. It is complete when fitted with a curb chain.

Round shank hackamore This bridle has rounded cheeks, with a movable, leather-covered steel cable noseband which will not drop over the nose. It gives the correct leverage and control without pinching in any way.

Improved hackamore This type has rounded cheeks and braided leather noseband over a bicycle-type chain. It is usually made of stainless steel.

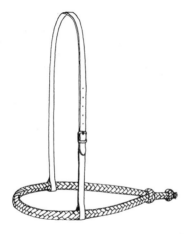

Bosal hackamore.

Bosal Unlike the above hackamores, the bosal is not a 'mechanical' bridle. It is simply made without the metal shanks of the mechanical bridles and usually has horsehair reins. The reins attach directly to the underside of the bosal, as the nosepiece is called. This is mainly a training bridle and may only be used in the show ring on horses under four years of age.

90

Western saddles

Western saddles are much heavier than English saddles. Modern designs vary a good deal, and some saddles may weigh as little as 20lb (generally, however, they weigh nearer 40lb). Traditionally they were designed to carry a person long distances, and very often the seats were padded for additional comfort. There are a number of seat designs, and a really good show saddle, with silver, may cost up to $2000 or more!

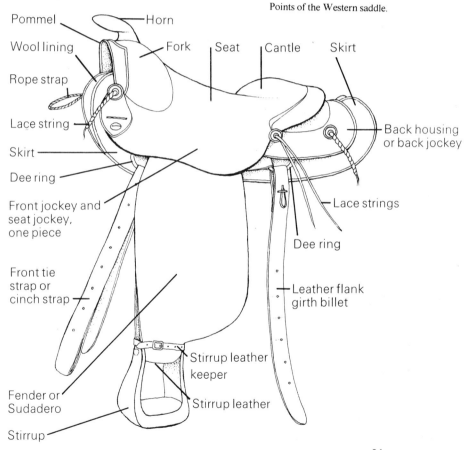

Points of the Western saddle.

Pommel

Horn

Wool lining

Fork

Seat

Cantle

Skirt

Rope strap

Lace string

Back housing or back jockey

Skirt

Dee ring

Front jockey and seat jockey, one piece

Lace strings

Dee ring

Front tie strap or cinch strap

Leather flank girth billet

Stirrup leather keeper

Fender or Sudadero

Stirrup leather

Stirrup

Western show bridles

These again come in many different and attractive styles, some rather elaborate and others very simple. Here it is a matter of personal choice as to which is most suitable.

Spotted bridle This is a fancy scalloped bridle. The throatlatch and reins are narrow, the throatlatch being $^1/_2$-in (12mm) wide and the reins $^3/_4$-in (18mm) wide. The bridle is black or dark brown in colour.

Diamond spotted parade bridle This is made of best quality bridle leather and is black in colour. It is decorated with diamond spots.

Narrow show bridle This is a very neat and simple design in quality leather. It is double stitched and is finished with stainless steel or preferably silver rosettes.

15 Clothing for the horse

Clothing for the horse consists primarily of rugs and bandages. The horse requires these for warmth and protection.

Bandages

There are several different types, each with its own job to do.

Stable bandage, with gamgee underneath.

The stable bandage is used in the stable or when travelling. It is made of wool, stockinette, flannel or felt, and is wrapped round the leg from below the knee down over the fetlock joint. Stable bandages are usually 7 or 8ft (2 or 2.5m) long and $4^1/_2$-in (11cm) wide. The purpose is to keep the legs warm and encourage circulation. When used for travelling they prevent the horse from injuring himself by knocking one leg against another.

Exercise bandages These are applied round the cannon bone, leaving the fetlock free, when the horse is working, to support the tendons or to protect the legs from injury. Exercise bandages are

made of crêpe or stockinette; they are shorter than stable bandages
– about 6ft (1.8m) long – and only $2^1/_2$-in (6cm) wide. All leg
bandages should be applied by an experienced person as they can
cause great damage if improperly wrapped.

The finished tail bandage.

Tail bandage This is used to improve the shape of the tail after it
has been 'pulled' and to protect it from being rubbed sore when
travelling. Great care must be taken not to leave the tail bandage on
too long or to wrap it too tight.

Rugs

Day rug Traditionally made of woollen material, its purpose is to
keep the horse warm when travelling or standing in the stable
during the day.

Night rug Traditionally made of jute lined with wool, its purpose is to
keep the horse warm and is primarily used in the stable at night.

Both day and night rugs are now available in a range of man-
made materials. They have the added advantage of being machine
washable and so tend to be more hygenic.

Blankets

These are used under the day rug or jute rug for extra warmth in
winter. Blankets are made of wool.

94

Leather roller This is used to keep the jute rug or day rug in place. The roller is padded to leave a clear channel along the horse's spine. Most United States blankets and sheets, and many in the UK as well, will have their own surcingle straps sewn on and may not require a roller, though arched rollers are preferable as they avoid the possibility of pressure on the withers and spine.

Jute roller This is made of the same material as the jute rug. The roller is padded to avoid pressure to the horse's spine and has two leather straps and buckles to fasten the roller.

Coloured rollers Some rollers are made to match day rugs; this is for appearance only. This type of roller must still be padded and will have two leather straps and buckles to fasten the roller in position. Personally, I have found that the amount of padding put in any of the above rollers is insufficient and it is usually better to use a piece of foam sponge under the roller to avoid unnecessary pressure on the spine.

New Zealand rug This is a waterproof rug traditionally made of canvas and lined with wool, and is worn by horses living out in the field under winter conditions. These rugs are also now made from tougher synthetic materials, and lined with acrylic fibre pile.

Summer sheet Normally made of cotton, it is used to keep the horse clean and free from dust in summer and to protect him from flies.

Anti-sweat rug Looking like a large string vest, this rug may be used after exercise when the horse is hot, to let him cool down slowly. It is also useful after hunting underneath a jute rug for horses that may break out in a sweat. The anti-sweat rug will allow the horse to dry out without catching a chill.

Quarter sheet These are used on exercise, mainly on Thoroughbred horses in very cold weather, to keep their loins and backs warm.